Bald Eagles

by Grace Hansen

Abdo
ANIMALS OF NORTH AMERICA
Kids

abdopublishing.com

Published by Abdo Kids, a division of ABDO, PO Box 398166, Minneapolis, Minnesota 55439.
Copyright © 2016 by Abdo Consulting Group, Inc. International copyrights reserved in all countries.
No part of this book may be reproduced in any form without written permission from the publisher.
Printed in the United States of America, North Mankato, Minnesota.

THIS BOOK CONTAINS
RECYCLED MATERIALS

102015
012016

Photo Credits: iStock, Shutterstock

Production Contributors: Teddy Borth, Jennie Forsberg, Grace Hansen

Design Contributors: Laura Mitchell, Dorothy Toth

Library of Congress Control Number: 2015941756
Cataloging-in-Publication Data

Hansen, Grace.
Bald eagles / Grace Hansen.
p. cm. -- (Animals of North America)
ISBN 978-1-68080-108-8 (lib. bdg.)
Includes index.
1. Bald eagle--Juvenile literature. I. Title.
598.9/43--dc23
2015941756

Table of Contents

Bald Eagles

Bald eagles live in the United States and Canada. They live in Mexico, too.

Bald eagles can be found near bodies of water. Lakes and coastlines are good places to spot them.

Bald eagles are covered in feathers. Their heads and tails are white. The rest of their bodies are brown.

Bald eagles have big yellow beaks. They have large **talons**.

Food & Hunting

Bald eagles use their **talons** to catch **prey**. They use their beaks to tear apart food.

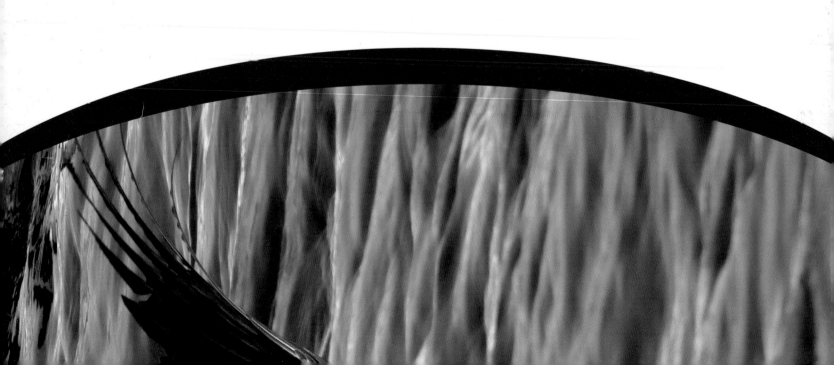

Bald eagles have great eyesight. This helps them spot **prey** from far away.

A bald eagle's favorite meal is fish. It will also eat small birds and rodents.

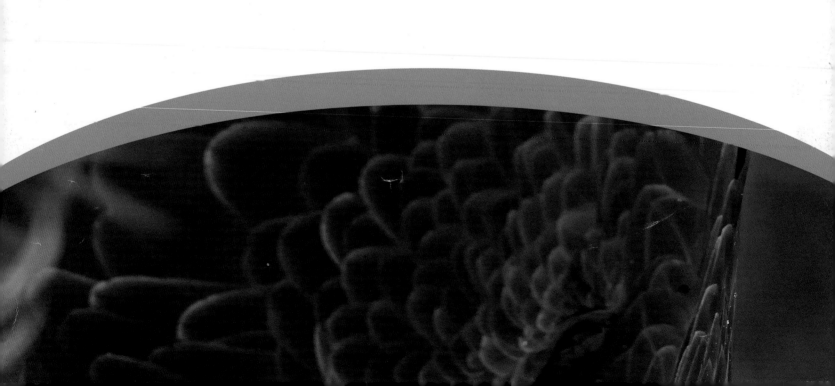

Baby Bald Eagles

A bald eagle stays with the same **mate** for life. They build a nest together. They build it high up in a tree. They use sticks and twigs.

Bald eagles return to the same nest each year. Females lay one to three eggs. Baby eagles are called chicks. Mothers care for their chicks for about 12 weeks.

More Facts

- Bald eagles can live up to 28 years in the wild.

- Young bald eagles are one color. They will get their white feathers when they are around five years old.

- There is only one bird larger than a bald eagle. It is a California condor.

Glossary

mate – one of a pair of animals that have offspring together.

prey – an animal hunted or killed for food.

talons – claws, especially on birds of prey.

Index

abdokids.com

Use this code to log on to abdokids.com and access crafts, games, videos, and more!

Abdo Kids Code:

ABK1088